D1405387

Gallery Books
Editor Peter Fallon

CARNIVAL MASKS

Seán Lysaght

CARNIVAL MASKS

Gallery Books

Carnival Masks
is first published
simultaneously in paperback
and in a clothbound edition
on 27 February 2014.

The Gallery Press
Loughcrew
Oldcastle
County Meath
Ireland

www.gallerypress.com

*All rights reserved. For permission
to reprint or broadcast these poems,
write to The Gallery Press.*

© Seán Lysaght 2014

ISBN 978 1 85235 586 9 *paperback*
       978 1 85235 587 6 *clothbound*

A CIP catalogue record for this book
is available from the British Library.

Contents

in memory of John Hurst

Skylarks in January

None since October,
and now there are four
calling across the clouds,
still dragging a grey hawser

that ends in the sea
after weeks in the links
while the waves poured thunder.
It's an early release

of that high, blinding obsession
with the sun's glare
to make every hill disappear
through the eye of a song

when all love wants —
there in the heather — is a nest,
a few stray notes,
a closer look at that crest.

Catkins

When February turns mild
 alder catkins expand,
yellow-green mills of gold
 that I disperse with my hand.

The hazels are finer,
 pale yellow tails
of tree-semen that find
 the deep crimson of the female.

Ah, this is the seed of the wind,
 which I scatter for you
wherever you touch or bend
 in the bright dew.

March Wind

Wind scours the bones of the living.
Mornings wake, bleary-eyed
from weeping the breezes.
Walls hold

but wind-noise still penetrates
to the core,
grinds back the comforts of myth
to the original rib.

Who are these, lighting their fire,
going through the motions of a day
with a wind pack
constantly worrying and tugging?

What would we say
to the stars of their eyes?
How could words cross
the tors of their teeth?

Clouds ride the blue
on an occasional sunny day,
snapping Kodak time back
to their anxious hearth

and, somehow,
a thrush does the job
of all creation
in its late winter station

attacking blustery dark
with reiterated song
and, through the abyss
of this relentless air,

a kestrel's double blade
is working the wind
so that the eye might anchor
a mind to the land,

hold down its clatter
of loose galvanized
on a shed where
some poor turf is husbanded.

Dated pages
litter the ditch,
a sheepdog keeps to its blown fur
and the crocus shivers

to offer saffron to the world.
Nothing now in cold blood
could ever be witness here
to stirring branches as they catch fire.

The Arrival of Swallows

Back in Mayo after an Italian winter
we have no more use for our carnival masks.
They lie redundant as spring comes into colour,
the long-regarded hedges suddenly vigorous.

Into the confusion of this deepening green
a hare runs, like a player offside,
caught between an eye that held the moon
and a pace that could lift the countryside,

always unexpected, at an angle
to the attitude of a big lonely house
where the owner guards an empty shell
against the excesses of the wilderness,

until the swallows showed up, that is,
winging it low, always switching the game.
The place they wanted back was this
drive, this very porch where they swept in

to chatter over the nests at last year's door
and start again by confounding every metaphor.

April Wind

The north-east is an unbidden guest,
a grumpy old man
whose shed is full of skylarks.

He scattered all the confetti
at Cherry's wedding
before the bride arrived,

and last night
he tipped over the garden chairs
and rained on an age
of novels and tea things.

He has every black crow
struggling back to veer
into a silver angle
where it could disappear.

Only those who know him could forgive him
lifting the skirts of the hedge,
whole lines of leaves
prepared elaborately for weeks
to face the other way.

But he can teach the rods of willow to bend
and get busy with wind fish,
and we love to watch
the blast of his airplane engines
silvering the pastures.

He's the only one who can get
the evergreen violins to play.
Look at his oak,
the branches worn thin

from all that conducting!
And still not a stitch on him!

Hare

Hare burdened with too much lore
down to the symbol for speed on my lawnmower
moves away in low gear ahead of the lights,

then finds a gap in the hedge
and is off for months, years,
across rushy hillsides and the outback of whins.

Hare stays clear of our conscience.
His absence intensifies
like evening mist over iris blades

when an energy snags in nets,
wattles divining, and they bundle
his terror into a bag of darkness.

Even greyhounds with muzzles
can't quite keep up
with his old role over furlongs

between lines of farmers
shouting for a hare's blood
like a wartime football crowd.

He spurns the law's release
to fling himself at derelict townlands,
recovers his form in long grass

where the air shines with cables
of abseiling spiders
and no storybook can reach him —

until sudden March snow
finds a group hunkered down by a ditch
at some early business

which our day breaks up, melts,
and then there are two travelling
along a field margin,

the hundred-year-old hedges
a new bother to their rights,
and then one

leaving cover
to cross an airfield runway
along a hare's continuing line

back to battlefields,
hauntings,
unsettling the high horses.

Five Hawks

The first is a commotion in the day
of fields, an explosion
of redwing and fieldfare,
starlings there in a tight flock
swerving on the glare.

The second echoes in all the pipits,
swings in its wing blades,
tracing loops above the house,
and slides away along its own line
to a solitude of wild land.

The third swoops into a vault
of thorns, but the hooded crows
take up position in their cloaks
and wait on fence posts
until it retreats.

The fourth is a magician,
its stage a hedge in the garden.
Its yellow eye commands
our wonder to the window
and makes the small birds vanish.

The fifth will not be written
as a sudden ghost at dusk,
a harrowing of twilight,
a gull cry in August over a shorn field.
It will exhaust all of these —

and then it appears.

Whimbrels

I thought it was wind round the house.
What else but the edge of stone
could conjure such a visitation
of strange notes and wild flutings?

I shifted through my rooms,
unsure of this enchantment,
as if being asked to believe the child
who had said a fairy was coming.

And then I saw whimbrels:
two May birds in my neighbour's field,
curlew cousins with stylish crowns
established in a waste of daisies and dock.

They were working worms out of the ground.
I watched them preening, their long bills
checking every tract of plumage
for the long flight north.

And when they left, they called over
the drumlins in fly-past, to exalt
the actual, like the coming of a queen.
The townland was full of wonderful noises.

17.5.2011

Hazelbrook

for Jan Stokes

I walked down the rushy townland
after wet weather,
each hoof-print in the poached ground
a cupful of clearing sky.

The culverts were shy.
Drains whispered as they gathered
to a stream that sank under the road,
hugging a gulley.

My walking followed,
but hazel boles closed ranks
to keep the channel back.
Tree flakes spun down the otter lane,

a flood poured into its own throat
of hart's tongue, and a rocky face
showed where falling water was strong.
Then the echoes softened to moss,

relaxed to minnow-instant,
beadings, eddies, spider cliffs.
I knew the river would have to leave
the smouldering fire of those willows.

It would not lift the silt of a well
kept for bucket-clank only.
A walled passage like a mill race
hurried the stream past her dreaming face,

and hurried surface bubbles
out of the shadows of clay and spleenwort

to break on what they had seen hidden
in the stalactites of roots.

We parted in a billiard green of open fields.
Water spread to a stony margin
where cattle drank the far horizon
out of a pool whose foam had spoken.

Old Willow

Old willow on a hill
with the sky in its hair
and the sun in its dapple of shadow —
so long structuring space,

so long waiting above the lake
in its lonely fort.
It keeps a hearth
of dust and wood bone

under the roar of leaves
and tends a small happiness
of grass and irises
instead of paradise.

The lower branches have caught
beards of fleece;
the belly is pure mahogany
polished by passing sheep.

Wool resin stays on wood
and on your feeling hands
that you raise now
to break a set of antlers —

but don't stay long.
Your lit world lives
by another agitation
and you must get on.

White Man

1 MY SILHOUETTE

My silhouette is a man-
shaped hole in the land.

I go past stones
and sky fallen on waters.

Do you need more proof?

When you saw me
stepping out of the office
in a glaring detonation,
autumn sun, you said.

No need for god.

2 AT CORRYLOUGH

My pure suit is so becoming;
here is too far for anything
to be borne from the world.

Do not confuse my example with freedom,
that arena where bodies are cleared
from the theatre of death.

Now that I am rid of everything
I have too much to lose
to delay for ordinary grief.

I will not be distracted by your pity.
Every step I take is counted within me,
told against the stones, the wind-moan.

3 DIANA

On my way back
from settling a land question,
a cascade crossed my trail
from a higher source.

Then a fence
led me on through spruce.
The first signs of her feet
were on glinting sand.

I crept along cresting water
to the heap of clothes by the furze.
The deep pool quivered and shifted
as if a salmon were passing.

And that was that.
Otherwise you disappear into the prize
and can't admire it,
your stag-mouth bellowing regret.

I had to exult
in the decorations I bore away:
red beads on the rowan,
royal fern in the sun.

4 ON STYLE

I was distracted by tinklings,
as I struggled with the harness
of the elaborate day.

They wanted me dreaming
mouse kingdoms,
spreadeagled under the soft
cover of owl-hoot,

to let myself fall
down a long dark shaft
among outlandish shapes
and hesitant, inquisitive forms.

But after all that,
daybreak is still skittish,
still a high, truculent horse
stretching the reins.

You have to walk the page
of last night's frost
to find him in the same place —
and get a grip.

How could we ever tackle dreams
without these comings and goings?

5 INKLINGS

White is the last fire,
the prism at the crater's rim
after the labour of schoolmen
grinding their ochre through the ages.

My inklings peer
into the turning of a shell
to reach the dog whelk's gland,
a dark gleam

stored like a warrior's cuirass
in the belly of a horse.
Fifty to a nib
is more than enough

for a purple line
to drag my rainbow colours
beyond the thorny ditch.
I am waiting here

for the treasure
of my own footprints
leaving a muddy lek
in the plumes of their breathing.

6 WHITE WOMAN

She moved over the moor
in a bridal gown and veil

making steady progress
among the banners of grass.

A dunlin flew past
like an alien's eye

following her line
with the crease of the river.

She diminished
to a speck in the glen —

if she screamed then
who would have heard her?

He would have heard her.
He was there already ahead

where sky and mountains
vanish on a point of desire —

white woman, white man,
out of earshot, abroad.

A Jay Feather

for Lynda

I know of a wood that hangs
like a heavy drape
flung over a hill in the midlands.

You can hear jays deep in its folds
tearing like engines
at the fabric of a winter's day.

Way down in the leaf litter,
beyond where it is normal
or decent for a walker to go,

there must be a fragment of that blue,
that eye through which you dive on a thread,
taking the whole day with you.

Rain at the Lake

Chimney smoke had been lazy all afternoon,
so when I went down with my rod
to the lake's solitude,
raindrops pecking at my chances
were a surprise.

They got bigger, till every one was jumping
in a ring of its own vanishing.

I stood in the hissing surface
till my shoulders were cold.

Then the drains were in full voice,
hunkered down at the hedges' base.
Water was loud in the land.
A dull seep at the upper end
was eight feet wide
in the fire of new irises,
swallowing ground,
toiling the flash of sky,
reworking clouds,
crashing into the marigolds.

Reedmace on their high lances
looked down at a surge flooding their ankles
but couldn't stop it.
Silt was being delivered
on winter's orders.

Farther out, the evening had cleared to a mirror.

A distant swimmer,
a pair of scissors through a bolt of silk,
headed his wake across, as straight as a plane.

Storm Petrels

Pilgrims at midnight,
our flashlamps climbing the stairs,
we had a scuffle with buffetings
on the last flight
and crept up on all fours
under the lid of the wind.

The enclosure steadied us.
Wall and corbelling
had been heaped for so long
chink by chink, we could not go wrong,
and the hutch of stone was heaviest
at the very top, to make us strong.

Darkness was a swarm
of darker fragments, of wills
briefly flickering in my beam.
These were said to be the souls
of dead monks coming home
on a gust to their star garden.

There was one, atop a wall,
trapped in the dazzle of our light!
He had dancing shoes for the sea,
little black webbed feet,
and each beaded eye of Biscay
shone with its original star.

To conquer this dark
another age painted terror —
but none was here.
I fingered the plumage gently
and blessed our reverent heads
with a motto: 'Never fear.
The boats are coming back.

This will be remembered
in a gurgle and a small click you hear
when you listen at the stone gap.'

Chirbling

for Jessica

A sound at the window
is house martins.
Their hive, their little hutch

a foot from the bedroom
measures twenty years
from Worcestershire.

All summer now
their business is set
from dawn chorus to dusk.

An airy life
at home above our site
catches flies all day,

traces the sky
with comings and goings.
This is your childhood,

a noise bubbling
under the eaves at twilight —
and now in Ireland.

A bat spins antiquity
all around the rooms
and our little rain-

forest elves
are settled in the nest,
still chirbling — your word.

Tarsaghaunmore in Late August

A squall at the mountain's heart
set the sea trout free
for one more run.
Foaming streams
washed over their dimples,
swallowed their tail-fins' applause.
The dead god of grilse,
freckled by midges and sea lice,
hung from a fence
in the shade of a pine.

Wind on the stones
calls our love home.

Heather was there in profusion
doing the flowers,
and swallows swept along
a river still in their keeping,
the store running low —
look at the sun's measure
sinking so early by eight!

Wind on the stones
calls our love home.

Old engines mark our defeat
with shattered pieces of salvage,
piping, flagstones, girders.
No one working a furnace,
no one left to beat out
the spangled feet we clattered on
when the road was first tarred.

Storm Diary

Wind from the east is a banshee wailing
at the door, from the west a howling chimney.
The worst nights, the car is tense as a cat.
The two of us are there at the centre
of force nines shaking the gate and rattling
the loose slates of our insistence:
we have made the right choice. Hours of telly,
journal entries, phone calls from outside
pass our time in the lighthouse with a query
(even as the whitethorns I planted knuckle
down and shy away from standing straight).
How many winters before our hearts are
twisted? And the wind answers: by the time
you know that, it will already be too late.

In Memory of My Father

Nead an chaislín thíos sa sceach,
uibheacha geala i bhfolach,
imeall néata fite fuaite
as spíonta géara is bláthanna caite.

Ar aon nós seo mar a shamhlaím é,
nead san aiteann nach bhfaca mé.
'Deacair an nead sin a aimsiú.
Ní féidir leat,' a dúirt tú.

Tusa a d'inis dom an scéal,
a chuir an gheis sin ar mo shaol.

2 A STONECHAT'S NEST

As you were slipping away
the yellow gorse was on show,
flowers and spines packed tight,
a smell of coconut in March.

And two lively stonechats
were there in my territory
flicking their tails,
flycatching like yo-yos,

Donacha an Chaipín
and Máirín na Triúise
knocking the pebbles together
of the latest news.

When I was beating the bush
of thorns and withered grass,

after a hidden clutch,
you would say how hard it was to find,

such was the knowledge you offered.
My fingers at full stretch
were scratched in the finest of lines
when they withdrew.

And there I stood again
at a brilliant wall of gorse
looking for a way through,
with birds all calling for you, of course.

3 YOUR LAST CAST

The car was unsteady on the stony track
as we advanced among the pillared ash
holding a June sky above bare limestone.
This was the Burren outpost at Lough Mask
that we had read about in Praeger's book.
My English friend was there as we'd arranged,
emerging from an undergrowth of scrub,
his hands opened on an offering of chanterelles.
That day, we came as anglers to the head
of the Cong canal, a deep rapid shift
of transparency over weeds and fish.
I handed you a rod for your last cast,
to honour those days when you were rod master
with everything on earth still to hope for.

Red Deal

Now I'm the curator of a winter sun
striking the panel of the kitchen door
in our new house. If the angle is low
you find red deal is true to its colour.
Five years ago I discovered the knot
glowing bright red at the thinnest cut.

Sonnets to a Tudor Poet

He pluckt a bough, out of whose rift there came
Small drops of gory blood, that trickled down the same.
— The Faerie Queene

1

A man I used to teach, a great surfer
who has done the waves off Smerwick Harbour,
gave me this jawbone from the massacre.
I have it in front of me as a challenge,
to suggest two teeth remaining along
a honeycomb, a worn alabaster flange.
Metaphors, no problem. Molars are stones
to step over the stream of time, the bone
is an obol under the thumb for Charon —
journeyman stuff! It does not tell how he cursed
in his Italian; his panic came
too late to be read back from the bone,
and yet this must be where my English starts,
this remnant of a garrison poleaxed.

2

An update from Italy: just last week
we had taken a twisting, climbing road
up to the pass at about four thousand feet.
Woodland gave way to rock and the blue air
of the Apennines. Crickets were milling heat.
Had those been goats or sheep in the clearing?
On the way back down, traffic had to stop,
and three herdsmen delivered the answer
with shouts and whistles above a tinkling
flock of mountain sheep in a stream across
our path. In a moment, it was over —
cars moved on, the herd was back in the cover
of groves where all those shepherds ever do
is talk in the tradition that launched you.

3

We have horses in the fields below the house
swishing the tail of an uneventful afternoon
among the thistles, as you must have known.
On windy days, when everything's beaten down,
they assemble as their own monument,
rumps to the wind — as we say *tóin le gaoth*.
I wonder if they suffered your stricture,
if you told the children to turn away
as mare and stallion tussled rampant
before coupling repeatedly where May
blossom thrived, as if Jove's 'lusty hed'
came down to earth at your managed hedge
and then in epic metre galloped off
among your sheep, scattering the flock.

4

If watching trees could make them grow,
these saplings would be mature oaks by now
to protect our house from the westerlies.
The readers of the skies told us the signs,
but we still built here despite the warnings
about wet winters and more severe storms,
just as you waved a flag in Tyrone's face.
Late July, the Severn has spread into the fields,
the Avon has risen, islanding the towns,
and inns are ruined where they sang your sweet Thames.
I take a break to look after my plantations
and see that the stems are safe from hares.
The winter nights here test all my cares
and shake my hopes to their foundations.

5

The walled town of Corke. 1594.
Your song has dreamed midsummer. The screech owl
has been quelled, the marriage bed is decked
with little cupids sporting round the posts
and an amber moon rising into space
has confirmed you both at your happiest.
Just then, two men stood in the street below
watching your lattice, and a feeble glow
wavering before you blew the taper out.
One had eaten his fill at your table.
The other was going to watch at the gate.
'How did it go for Lady Elizabeth
and Master Edmund?' 'The wedding went well,
but everything they have is so fragile.'

6

There are no signs for the last miles to your
monument in Ireland. I had to ask for
Spenser's castle and found they knew your name
and so allowed my trespass over two fields
of deep, tedded hay. The light of August
was ebbing around your 'ruine of time'.
A mob of swallows chased a sparrowhawk
that had just left the cliff of your old house.
I squeezed in through a broken gate and climbed
your winding stair to an emptiness, an epic
imagined where predators now came to pluck
their kill. Going down, I raised another ghost,
a kestrel from an arch and heard it calling
over lonely flats at the Awbeg's margin.

A Venetian Notebook

Before I left for Venice I didn't enjoy fishing,
being stuck in a boat all day — but at least I was practising.

At Shannon departures, in the queue to check in,
I see a woman with Dante's nose where Italy begins.

I'm fifty when I get here, arriving at night
well after sundown, so I go on by moonlight.

I can't be bothered with maps, so I'm following my wife.
This works for me in Venice, but it's difficult in life.

The middle class of Europe are a funny lot.
They stay north in winter and come south when it's too hot.

In an alleyway I pass a limping gondolier,
unsure if his element were land or water.

The shop owner waits like a spider for a fly.
His window is a web to catch the tourist's eye.

Where I grew up, the salmon men used a gandelow;
I rhyme their boat with gondola.

I take a further liberty: their boats are *naomhógs*,
and the city of Venice is one big *crannóg*.

This Grand Canal is Kavanagh's shade of green
with villas at the edge and boat-traffic in between.

Avant-garde forms are types of human freedom.
The risks the artist took are what they have in common.

This shop is selling second-hand books by weight —
an object lesson in the slim volume's fate.

The mourners are in costume as they load the hearse:
lords, ladies and fools in sixteenth-century dress.
They stop for a moment as the boatman leaves alone
and then a fool starts chatting on his mobile phone.

My parents come to Italy now that they are dead,
still the same people travelling in my head,
but more vivid, enhanced, if they appear in a dream,
like my mother's radiant face when I arrive home.

The café crowds are clapping under the moon
as the players finish, having called the world's tune.

When my great-uncle, a seminarian, died in Rome
my father found his bird-notes in the attic at home.

Somewhere here, as he stepped out of a boat,
the waters of Lethe washed over Goethe's foot.

When dining in Venice, if you want to be fleeced,
go to the places where great writers used to eat!

I'm stuck in a gallery, but my wife wants to eat.
What I desperately need is take-away art!

Wolf whistles all day long in the flat
from a caged parrot in a window opposite.

The line of my feet along a deserted quayside
can only be written once I get back into the shade.

People are milling round at the opening of a show
of erotic art, among paintings and photos.
One artist has his model with him in a see-through dress.
Although I may look like a critic, I'm trying to guess

if she has anything on under it, and I don't think so.
He'll ruin the trade in pictures, I think it's wrong
of this Botticelli to bring Venus along.
We can all like peaches, but we like to believe
that our taste for still life has a higher motive.

All these damned pigeons! My bird of peace
would be a peregrine falcon to clear the place.

Venice is romantic if you like lying in a boat
with tourists on a bridge taking pictures of you both.

At San Giorgio Maggiore, two things I recognize:
the sea spitting hopelessly at the Catholic franchise.

When the great plague came to an end
it had killed fifty thousand Venetians,
so the city built this church to honour the Redeemer
and never blamed him for not ending it sooner.

Palladio's church is classically pure,
but the crucified Saviour still hangs there.

When RTE showed Visconti's film with Aschenbach at the Lido
there was outrage, and an editorial in *The Limerick Leader*.

Vacanze at the Lido, a vacancy: just sand
by the sea, waves breaking in front of the cabins.
My freckles and white skin enter this space
among the young ones as I submit to a test,
which I pass once I'm in. There are not many
bathers. The breeze makes the water as choppy as Kerry.

In the Jewish quarter today. I only made it
out of an old family bookdealing habit,

following directions to an English shop.
Ours was in a basement, where we traded hope
for the poor. A woman asks for *The Merchant from Ennis*
and I show her. 'Is that the one by Shakespeare?' 'Yes.'
A generation later, my path is still
paved with the proceeds of that humble till.

Floating in the Grand Canal: a feathered wing.
Despite Renaissance, the gods are still littering.

We're both northerners here, which makes a change.
If it's borders you want, try the Alpine range.

Our meal in the restaurant is disturbed by thunder:
a sudden commotion, then a small form on the tiled floor
comes to rest at my rucksack. Startled by an owl,
I recognize the real thing before Athene's symbol.

Do You Know the Land Where Lemons Grow?

from the German of Goethe

Do you know the land where lemons grow,
and golden oranges glow in rich leaves?
A gentle wind blows from a cloudless sky,
the myrtle is quiet and the laurel grows high —
do you know it?
        That's where I'd like to move
with you, my loved one.

Do you know the house with its roof on pillars?
The great hall is bright, everything shimmers,
and marble figures stand and watch me there:
what have they done to you, you poor creature?
Do you know it?
        That's where I'd like to move
with you, my guardian.

Do you know the mountain and the cloudy pass?
The mule finds his footholds in the mist.
An ancient race of dragon lives in caves,
and a waterfall shoots down from towering cliffs.
Don't you know it?
        Father, that's where our path runs,
let's get going!

Autumn Day

from the German of Rainer Maria Rilke

Lord, it is time. Summer was a huge space.
Lay your shadow now on the sundials
and in the lowlands let the winds loose.

The last fruits will ripen at your sign.
With two more southern days in your correction,
compel them on to their mature perfection
and send the last sweetness into the swollen vine.

It's too late now to start to build a house.
The lonely heart will keep its unsold wares,
will stay awake, will read, will write long letters
for many days, and still not find peace,
as dead leaves blow along the thoroughfares.

Sea Song

Capri. Piccola Marina

from the German of Rainer Maria Rilke

Timeless commotion off the sea,
sea wind at night:
not coming here for anyone.
When someone stays awake
he has to see
how you can be endured:
timeless commotion off the sea,
blowing as if only
for the element of stone,
pure space
rushing in from a distance . . .

O how you are known
to a swaying fig tree
up there in the light of the moon.

Archaic Torso, Apollo

from the German of Rainer Maria Rilke

We never knew his unperceiving head
which held the ripening apples of his eyes.
Like a sconce, the torso radiates instead
of his gaze, and in it we surmise

them, steady and intense. Otherwise, how could the span
of chest delight you and, as the hips
turned slowly, why did a smile come to your lips
at that middle point of generation?

Otherwise, this were merely a stub of damaged boulder
under the frail lintel of the shoulders.
It would not shimmer like a leopard's fur,

it would not radiate beyond its frame
just like a star, not a point anywhere
that does not see you; your life will have to change.

Jessica and the Butterfly

I call this our haven: a garden
high in wooded hills,
the ridges of a warm autumn.
The tiny kites of red admirals

glide in sunlit space
between a tall cedar and our door.
Hornets blunder over the terrace
or crawl along the floor

to find another fallen grape.
(There was a good harvest
but we were three weeks late.)
Occasionally, there's a chase

when a hornet drives a butterfly
away from the yellowing vine.
The bells of the local sanctuary
keep striking time

like an anvil every half hour
but you are so settled in the shade
with your book and chair
you will not be disturbed.

I watch a butterfly on your hat,
a set of marbled wings
give its signal, open and shut,
then take off over the lawn's definition

to orbit once more
between the bells and grumpy hornets.
And I tell you that you are
this butterfly's favourite.

You didn't see it land,
but it comes back again
and perches on your hand
to be examined.

'It must think I'm a flower,' you say.
Although your hat is woven
from straw, and your dress is plain grey,
at this moment in the garden
it is you the butterfly has chosen.

Self-portrait at a Swimming Pool

A straw panama, a branded shirt,
white trousers, a pair of sandals,

almost everything surrendered
to the water in its blue basin,

the glare established as a star
on the visor of his eye-wear.

No books or magazines in this heat.
There's nothing for the heart to do.

A net has already cleared out
spiders and insects

and lies across the deck
after the nightly tribute.

Then he takes a plunge
into his own commotion

with everyone else away,
unsteadies the edge, makes spray

while there is time
between bells and the next flight.

A blue, inflatable dolphin
and a pink li-lo

are drifting aimlessly in sun
beside the white man.

Tuscan Landscape

This walled village is a high ship
on a journey through a sea of trees.
Every afternoon a buzzard soars lazily above the ridges.
From the terrace you glimpse a road
sinking through foliage and wild boar territories.
The tart staccato of hunters' guns
punctuates fine mornings.
                                        The scene
is perfect for the mind's easel, especially
when light flares at sunset
in the high trees, things are
reunited, the day takes on a shape
you could believe you have created.

Then, from a close corner,
at first low, then unmistakable,
a woman's sobbing drifts slowly,
like a smoke of mist in the treetops.

Here's a tribute that is also paid,
striking at your heart, because it's been there.

Olive Grove in Autumn

A lazy smoke uncoils
from a heap of cuttings,
dragging its train
through the branches as it goes.

Bees check for leftovers,
warblers try a few bars
of an old tune
as the premises empties.

The ground is being cleared
for a ceremony — how else
could a monarch as old as this
pass the time?

He thought he would inherit sooner,
and dash like a deer
ahead of their guns,
but he had to wait too long.

You can see the scars
of his amputations, the limbs
he lost in the wars.
Nothing now but to act

his age in these boles,
to be antiquity itself
while the shock of his hair
keeps growing the parasite

he breeds by pure accident —
nothing to do with him —
but it brings his people riches,
so he tolerates them

at their ritual
every November, beating
the oil grub out of him.
He pretends it's only the wind.

After Rain in Italy

From the high rib of a footbridge
over a deep ravine,
I look down on years
being poured over a weir
into a foaming furnace,

all the time wondering
if the ground is shaking
or if what I'm hearing
is memory stirring.

The Shannon at Limerick,
where my uncle paddled the rapids
in his gandelow before the war,
the first time anyone had dared,
and people applauded.

The stream at Knockbrack,
in Hartnett country.
My Devon minnow snatched a trout
from the muddy brew of a March spate.

An angler on the Rhône at Geneva
steered his line through the clear depths
of our early happiness
as she joked, taking his fish for a walk.

The Neckar was a grey canal
slipping away from Stuttgart,
where Beckett said,
there was nothing to report.

But now a heavy mane at the sill
is clean as the sea,

smashing water thundering on earth,
the sound coming free of rocks and leaves,

the measure of a lifetime
keeping a stable for Neptune.

His horses ran all night on the ridges
and now they come charging back
from a god's tour of the valley
on the surf of their glittering track.

Dorothy at Goslar

Winter was locked in the walls of Goslar
as tight as the judgements of that town
when she emphasized the word *Schwester*.

Snowflakes from the dull loom of cold
spread a cloth through the oakwoods
to catch the fall of each leaf

in the cradle of its shadow.
Only she could live on so little.
She kept a book to tell William

how the full moon sailed, or how snow
collapsed like meteors from the heaped trees.
Memory. A stove they could afford to feed.

She watched his brow in the firelight
through a new verb, *nachsinnen*, to brood.
The woman was from Blois, there was a daughter —

but Cumbria's lakes offered a page of ice
for him to make a fresh start
with skates borrowed from childhood.

He would spin free under the constellations,
and this would set like a doctrine in her eyes,
as hard as frosted stars.

Her love took on a different name that night
when the drifts were piling high.
He watched her tiny feet making tracks

back to innocence and never intervened.
Her loyalty would be like the wind
blowing over a hare's trail to leave no trace.

Tellaro

Pine trees welcome the road to Tellaro,
pulling its loops along the steep groves
of this coast, like a hose for water
to the villas, keeping the palette rich
with citrus trees, olive trees,
hibiscus and bougainvillea.

Privilege clings here like a lizard to a rock,
its tail washed by the sea,
its tongue of few words saying
'Private Property', 'Keep Clear'.

I stopped under a pergola
littered with flames of fallen leaves
where I couldn't tell if the swirling
was because of me or a wind of autumn
and I heard spring in its last speech
from a warbler in a green back yard
at home with its scratchy song.
The cycads held winter suspended in their fronds.

Above the cove the village roofs
kept well below my view,
husbanding a darkness,
packed so tight that only a few
holm oaks could find room in the square
and a narrow stone trough
confined agave — a burst of turquoise.

Just one silhouette floated in the blue afternoon.
A fisherman bent over twinkling water
had the whole stage of sea to himself
to draw the fish of the sun
along the fabulous, inexhaustible
line of the wide Mediterranean.

The Bay of Angels

for Elizabeth and John Montague

After the first, a second life stares
out here across the Bay of Angels
under the sun's blue eyes. The blue waters
come ashore all day to offer themselves
endlessly in every wave that rises.
Every mane of glass curls before it falls
to a final gesture, a rush of foam
falling back with a sigh from its metronome.

The elemental line was founded here
by the haunted practitioners of art.
They drove these dusty roads in the twenties
where the strict courtesy of a plaque
remembers life as a brilliant gesture.
One time we were happy with this remark
but now we want to follow down the cool
tiling of white steps and enter the pool.

There are few signs of whatever we have been:
a crumpled bathrobe on a ledge, a pair
of sandals left at the edge of a scene,
clues put in discreetly by the painter,
with some pathos in the way they were worn
to indicate the life of the bather,
our only weakness, like Achilles, at the heel,
a mark in leather to prove that this is real.

This coast has its proper tone of feeling;
it has mastered every interference known,
gone through whatever grief or rage could bring
to reach this space with a horizon.
Other stages are spread for suffering
but a mute decorum rules this one.

All it expects of us is that we pay
for time to keep disturbance away.

A tumbling coast with orange and lemon trees
and ancient olives is offered on this basis,
that we have lived enough with pieties,
or at least muddled through in other places
to come here with a harvest of leaves
to look over, admiring the traces
of a path to an archway, a garden, a door,
and the one room we spent years working for.

Notes and Acknowledgements

I should like to thank the editors of the following publications, where many of these poems were first published: *can can*, *The Irish Times*, *New Hibernia Review*, *North Munster Antiquarian Journal*, *Poetry Ireland Review*, *Revival*, *Stony Thursday Book* and *THE SHOp*.

'Jessica and the Butterfly' was first published in *La Paume Ouverte: A Festschrift for Françoise Connolly*, edited by Theo Dorgan (Poetry Ireland, 2010).

'Storm Petrels' was written following a visit to Skellig Michael in June 2009 and appeared in *Voices at the World's Edge*, edited by Paddy Bushe (Dedalus Press, 2010).

'Skylarks in January', 'Five Hawks' and 'Chirbling' were published in *The Lighter Craft: Poems for Peter Denman*, edited by Chris Morash and Kevin Honan (Astrolabe Press, 2013).

I should again like to thank Martin Evans, whose house in Italy has felt like home on many occasions over the past ten years.